PENGUIN BOOKS

dad
xxoo

To my wonderful Dad!
Thank you for everything
loads of love
Sally xxx

dad
xxoo

PENGUIN BOOKS

A truly rich man is one whose children run into his arms when his hands are empty.

Anon

But fair for me thou wert, O little life,
Fruitless, the fruit of mine own flesh, and blind,
More than much gold, ungrown, a foolish flower.
For silver nor bright snow nor feather of foam
Was whiter, and no gold yellower than thine hair,
O child, my child; and now thou art lordlier grown,
Not lovelier, nor a new thing in mine eyes.

Algernon Charles Swinburne, *Atalanta in Calydon*

A father is very miserable who has no other hold on his children's affection than the need they have of his assistance, if that can be called affection.

Montaigne

A chip off the old block.

John Milton

He that hath a wife and children, hath given hostages to fortune.

Francis Bacon

Clap hands, clap hands
Till father comes home
For father's got money
But mother's got none.
Clap hands, Daddy's coming
Up the wagon way
With his pockets full of money
And his hands full of clay.

Nursery rhyme

I am pleased to be praised by a man
so praised as you, father.

Cicero

It is a wise child who knows his own father.

Homer

Children are the poor man's riches.

Proverb

Daughters can never take too much care of their father.

Plautus

Fathers should be neither seen nor heard;
that is the only proper basis for family life.

Oscar Wilde

For a great sin a slight submission is sufficient in a father's eyes.

Terence

Full fathom five thy father lies
Of his bones are coral made
Those are pearls that were his eyes
Nothing of him that doth fade
But doth suffer a sea change
Into something rich and strange.

William Shakespeare, *The Tempest*

But by your father's worth if yours you rate,
Count me those only who were good and great.

Alexander Pope

He whose father is judge, goes safe to his trial.

Proverb

Hush little Baby, don't say a word,

Daddy's gonna buy you a mocking bird.

If that mocking bird don't sing,

Daddy's gonna buy you a diamond ring.

If that diamond ring turns to brass,

Daddy's gonna buy you a looking glass.

If that looking glass gets broke,

Daddy's gonna buy you a billy goat.

If that billy goat don't pull,

Daddy's gonna buy you a cart and bull.

If that cart and bull turn over,

Daddy's gonna buy you a dog named Rover.

If that dog named Rover don't bark,

Daddy's gonna buy you a horse and cart.

If that horse and cart fall down,

You'll still be the bestest baby in town.

Nursery rhyme

Thou art the framer of my nobler being;
Nor does there live on virtue in my soul,
One honourable hope, but calls thee father.

Samuel Taylor Coleridge

He that honoureth his father shall have a long life.

Apocrypha (Sirach)

Blessed indeed is the man who hears
many gentle voices call him father!

Lydia Maria Child

My father died a month ago
And left me all his riches;
A feather bed, and a wooden leg,
And a pair of leather breeches.
He left me a teapot without a spout,
A cup without a handle,
A tobacco pipe without a lid,
And half a farthing candle.

Nursery rhyme

A man doesn't shoot himself when he's going to be made a lawful father for the first time, unless he can see a long way into the future.

Henry Lawson

It was as good as a play to see his father with the children, but such a play as brings smiles with tears behind.

John Galsworthy

One father is enough to govern one hundred sons,
but not a hundred sons one father.

Proverb

I'll meet the raging of the skies,
But not an angry father.

Thomas Campbell

As the field, so the crops; as the father, so the sons.

Proverb

Put everything second to a father's opinion. It is for this that men pray to have obedient children in their homes, to pay back evil to their father's enemy and honour his friend as he does.

Sophocles

Bye, baby bunting,
Daddy's gone a-hunting,
Gone to get a little rabbit skin,
To wrap the baby bunting in.

Nursery rhyme

Any man can be a father,
but it takes a special person to be a dad.

Anon

CASABIANCA

The boy stood on the burning deck
Whence all but he had fled;
The flame that lit the battle's wreck,
Shone round him o'er the dead.

The flames roll'd on – he would not go
Without his Father's word;
That father, faint in death below,
His voice no longer heard.

Mrs Felicia D. Hemans

The words that a father speaks to his children in the privacy of home are not heard by the world, but, as in whispering galleries, they are clearly heard at the end, and by posterity.

Jean Paul Richter

Look! how he laughs and stretches out his arms,
And opens wide his blue eyes upon thine,
To hail his father; while his little form
Flutters as winged with joy. Talk not of pain!
The childless cherubs well might envy thee
The pleasures of a parent!

Lord Byron, *Cain*

MY AIN COUNTRIE

I am far frae my hame,
an' i'm weary aften whiles,
For the longed-for hame-bringing
an' my Father's welcome smiles.

Mary Lee Demarest

Thy father's merit sets thee up to view,
And shows thee in the fairest point of light,
To make thy virtues, or thy faults, conspicuous.

Joseph Addison, *Cato*

By the time a man realises that maybe his father was right, he usually has a son who thinks he's wrong.

Charles Wadsworth

TO MY FATHER

It matters not that Time has shed
His thawless snow upon your head,
For he maintains, with wondrous art,
Perpetual summer in your heart.

William Hamilton Hayne

If I chance to talk a little wild, forgive me;
I had it from my father.

William Shakespeare, *Henry VIII*

To her the name of father was another name for love.

Fanny Fern (Sara Payson Willis Parton)

When I was a boy of fourteen, my father was so ignorant I could hardly stand to have the old man around. But when I got to be twenty-one, I was astonished at how much the old man had learned in seven years.

Mark Twain

A father is someone who carries pictures where his money used to be.

Anon

Be kind to thy father, for when thou were young, who loved thee so fondly as he? He caught the first accents that fell from thy tongue, and joined in thy innocent glee.

Margaret Courtney

Leontine: An only son, sir, might expect more indulgence.
Croaker: An only father, sir, might expect more obedience.

Oliver Goldsmith

It is impossible to please the whole world
and your father as well.

Jean de la Fontaine

Little children are like arrows in the hands of the giant, and blessed is the man that hath his quiver full of them.

The Book of Psalms 127: 5

A man's children and his garden both reflect the amount of weeding done during the growing season.

Anon

A wise son maketh a glad father: but a foolish son is the heaviness of his mother.

The Book of Proverbs 10: 1

We think our fathers fools, so wise we grow.
Our wiser sons, no doubt will think us so.

Alexander Pope

The child is father of the man;
And I could wish my days to be
Bound each to each by natural piety.

William Wordsworth

The joys of parents are secret, and so are their griefs and fears: they cannot utter the one, nor they will not utter the other.

Francis Bacon

It is not flesh and blood, but heart which makes us fathers and sons.

Johann Friedrich von Schiller

When a father gives to his son, both laugh;
when a son gives to his father, both cry.

Jewish proverb

Children wish fathers looked but with their eyes;
fathers that children with their judgement looked;
and either may be wrong.

William Shakespeare

It is yourself that you see in your children: their bosoms are the safe repository of even the whispers of your mind: they are the great and unspeakable delight of your youth, the pride of your prime of life, and the props of your old age. They proceed from that love, the pleasures of which no tongue or pen can adequately describe, and the various blessings which they bring are equally incapable of description.

William Cobbett, *Advice to Young Men*

The character and history of each child may be a new and poetic experience to the parent, if he will let it.

Margaret Fuller, *Summer on the Lakes*

Through the survival of their children, happy parents are able to think calmly, and with a very practical affection, of a world in which they are to have no direct share.

Walter Pater

Noble fathers have noble children.

Euripides

A father is a banker given by nature.

French proverb

He only dies half who leaves an image of himself in his sons.

Carlo Goldoni

Fathers are blind to the faults of their daughters.

Anon

THE LITTLE BOY LOST

Father! Father! where are you going?
O do not walk so fast.
Speak, father, speak to your little boy,
Or else I shall be lost.

William Blake

I perceive affection makes a fool
Of any man too much the father.

Ben Jonson, *Every Man in His Humour*

You are the bows from which your children are sent forth.

Kahlil Gibran

THE FARMER AND HIS SONS

A father, being on the point of death, wished to be sure that his sons would give the same attention to his farm as he himself had given it. He called them to his bedside and said, 'My sons, there is a great treasure hid in one of my vineyards.' The sons, after his death, took their spades and mattocks and carefully dug over every portion of their land. They found no treasure, but the vines repaid their labour by an extraordinary and superabundant crop.

Aesop

The most important thing a father can do for his children is to love their mother.

Henry Ward Beecher

We are the buffoons of our children.

Pietro Aretino

Where parents do too much for their children, the children will not do much for themselves.

Elbert Hubbard

But the man, and especially the father, who is not fond of babies; who does not feel his heart softened when he touches their almost boneless limbs; when he sees their little eyes first begin to discern; when he hears their tender accents; the man whose heart does not beat truly to this test, is, to say the best of him, an object of compassion.

William Cobbett, *Advice to Young Men*

Dance to your daddy,
My little babby,
Dance to your daddy,
my little lamb;
You shall have a fishy
In a little dishy,
You shall have a fishy
When the boat comes in.

Nursery rhyme

COME HOME FATHER

Father, dear father, come home with me now,
The clock in the steeple strikes one.
You promised, dear father, that you would come home
As soon as your day's work was done.
Hear the sweet voice of the child,
Which the night-winds repeat as they roam.
Oh! who could resist this most plaintive of prayers:
 Please Father, dear father, come home.

Henry Clay Work

The girls gave their hearts into their mother's keeping, their souls into their father's, and to both parents, who lived and labored so faithfully for them, they gave a love that grew with their growth and bound them tenderly together by the sweetest tie which blesses life and outlives death.

Louisa May Alcott, *Little Women*

PENGUIN

Published by the Penguin Group
Penguin Group (Australia)
250 Camberwell Road, Camberwell, Victoria 3124, Australia
(a division of Pearson Australia Group Pty Ltd)
Penguin Group (USA) Inc.
375 Hudson Street, New York, New York 10014, USA
Penguin Group (Canada)
90 Eglinton Avenue East, Suite 700, Toronto, Ontario, Canada M4P 2Y3
(a division of Pearson Penguin Canada Inc.)
Penguin Books Ltd
80 Strand, London WC2R 0RL, England
Penguin Ireland
25 St Stephen's Green, Dublin 2, Ireland
(a division of Penguin Books Ltd)
Penguin Books India Pvt Ltd
11 Community Centre, Panchsheel Park, New Delhi – 110 017, India
Penguin Group (NZ)
67 Apollo Drive, Mairangi Bay, Auckland 1310, New Zealand
(a division of Pearson New Zealand Ltd)
Penguin Books (South Africa) (Pty) Ltd
24 Sturdee Avenue, Rosebank, Johannesburg 2196, South Africa
Penguin Books Ltd, Registered Offices: 80 Strand, London, WC2R 0RL, England

First published by Penguin Group (Australia), 2005

10 9 8 7 6 5 4 3

Text selection copyright © Penguin Group (Australia) 2005
Photographs pp. 1, 5, 9, 13, 21, 25, 29, 33, 37, 45, 49, 57, 61, 69, 73, 77, 81, 85, 89 Getty Images
pp. 17, 41, 53 APL/Corbis
pp. 65 photolibrary.com

Cover and text design by Claire Tice © Penguin Group (Australia)
Cover photograph by Getty Images
Printed in China by Everbest Printing Co. Ltd

ISBN-13: 978 0 143 00430 1
ISBN-10: 0 143 00430 1

www.penguin.com.au